Conscious Blue

poems

Veronica Schorr

Finishing Line Press
Georgetown, Kentucky

Conscious Blue

Copyright © 2021 by Veronica Schorr
ISBN 978-1-64662-637-3 First Edition
All rights reserved under International and Pan-American Copyright Conventions. No part of this book may be reproduced in any manner whatsoever without written permission from the publisher, except in the case of brief quotations embodied in critical articles and reviews.

ACKNOWLEDGMENTS

Grateful acknowledgement is made to *Long River Review*, in which "Because even Titanic sunk" first appeared.

I am forever grateful for the support and advice of my extraordinary mentors, friends, and family; there are too many of you to list here. Special thanks to V. Penelope Pelizzon and Bruce Cohen. Thank you to my dear friends Isabella Saraceni and Jenna Rubin. Thanks to my mom for… everything. To the team at Finishing Line Press: thank you for giving my poetry its first perfect bound home. And endless thanks to Jess—always the better poet of the two of us—for laughing at my puns.

* * *

Some italicized sections of "Kobudai" are borrowed from narration by Sir David Attenborough in Episode 1 of BBC's *Blue Planet II*.

The title "Wicked City" is taken from dialogue in chapter 4 of *The Bell Jar* by Sylvia Plath.

"Ode to Blue" was inspired by Claudia Rankine's *Citizen*.

Publisher: Leah Huete de Maines
Editor: Christen Kincaid
Cover Art: Isabella Saraceni
Author Photo: Isabella Saraceni
Cover Design: Julie Schorr

Order online: www.finishinglinepress.com
also available on amazon.com

Author inquiries and mail orders:
Finishing Line Press
PO Box 1626
Georgetown, Kentucky 40324
USA

Contents

ONE
Kobudai / 1
You've Reached the Dykes / 2
Keep It Simple, Stupid / 3
So Mark from work / 4
Iteration (I) / 6
Piazza della Signoria / 7

TWO
Café con Leche / 9
Dirty Laundry / 11
Tradycja / 12
Zero Beach / 13
Berlin / 14
Iteration (II) / 15
Erasure / 16
The girl becoming a woman knocks over the ketchup / 17
Wicked City / 19

THREE
Ode to Blue / 22

FOUR
Conscious Blue / 26
Grapefruit / 29
Iteration (III) / 30
Because even Titanic sunk / 31
Don't Tell Me It's Cliché / 32
Pastoral / 33
Self-Portrait / 34
You've Reached the Dykes II / 35

Let me escape my own insistence.
—Ellen Bass, *Indigo*

Kobudai

A pod of bottlenose dolphins is visiting a coral reef in the Red Sea. They skim their slender, slippery bellies over the coral methodically. *They've discovered coral with a mucous membrane that can protect them from infection.* It feels to them how it feels when your slim fingertips press one of my temples, then the other, pause for a kiss: connect the dots of stress.

Earlier tonight, on line for the bar, a voice says, loudly, *He's such a faggot.* No heads turn but mine. His friends laugh. If other throats itch and swell with an urge to defend the invisible he, I will never know. I observe how the voice's owner stands: arms crossed over a protruding chest, shoulders back, attempting to take up more space than his barely five-foot-three figure manages. It's as though I'm alone in my nook of a living room, watching this exchange take place on t.v.—like I am cold, somehow, even burrowed under two blankets with the thermostat set to seventy-five.

Nature confirms my belief that we are a species rare and lonely as the kobudai, a fish that can transform from female to male, passing the genes of the strongest females on to hundreds of offspring. *Of all the animals, fish are sexually the most fluid.* One slowly grows a more bulbous forehead, blue scaly spine, rows of acute new teeth. Extending his altered jaw, he dares the male who tried to mate with him before to fight back and the fish begin turning together, around and around, each striking the other's huge, rounded chin.

My favorite green t-shirt is completely soaked through. The print of Steve Irwin grappling with a crocodile is darkened and wrinkled and I reek of chlorine. I watch the sun dimly disappear behind a cloud and hear my uncle laughing with my older cousins, the sliding glass door to the porch closing behind them.

Mount Everest could disappear inside the Marianas Trench. That kind of lonely. Or when my uncle held me upside-down by the ankles, my nine-year-old neck submerged, tense; a green sea turtle with its head caught in a plastic bag, drowning in the same water it breathes.

The kobudai swims by, skimming the bottom of the pool with its sickly blue light pollution. I can't touch it, but I can finally see it now, watching with its bulging eyes.

You've Reached the Dykes
with Jessica Aloi

On second thought a wraparound porch seems racist.
I mean sure, we'll have rainbow pinwheels &
vegetarian barbecues, but it'll still be lily-white
& on the beach.

We'll drink out of pineapples on the lawn
just for shits
or better yet get married.

I'll poison the seagulls,
you'll sneak a dachshund home & hide her
so I open the door to slobbery kisses on dainty legs.

I'm thinking a raspberry bathroom
with vagina-pink backsplash?
Maybe salamander shutters & a flowerpot stereo
in every goddamn room.

When we argue over the puppy's name or whether
white tulips go in orange window baskets,
you'll storm out the screen door
into our herb garden.

& when it rains we'll spend the day drinking merlot,
not knowing what it is to feel small in a large world without each other.

Keep It Simple, Stupid

My dad used to skip gym class and go to the diner:
grilled cheese with ham, fries, side of gravy
a vanilla milkshake if he was hungover

Generations upon generations
sitting, slippery on red vinyl swapping
spit, stories, cigarettes, sweat,
never even looking at the menu.

Above the greasy Formica counter
the black hands of the obsolete clock read 2 a.m.
a mop swishes by
too
slowly

"Cheryl" stares blankly with her hairspray
mountain and purple clacking nails,
both of us aiming our impatience at you.

It's a diner,
I say with a faked, your-indecision-is-adorable smile,
just order something simple.

He barely finished high school, never went to college,
divorced once, married my mom, bankrupted us,
taught me nothing
is more delicious than dipping fries in your milkshake.

Instead of ordering you stare at me
like a stupid goldfish,
eyes wide mouth gasping for
words. I swallow my milkshake,
the sweaty glass forming a ring on my unopened menu.

So Mark from work

(you know, annoying kid—always
pushing me to get dinner with him)
asked me what keeps me up at night.

This complete existential fucking crisis of a question
cements my un-ergonomic chair to me
without warning
as if it wasn't super presumptuous of him to think that I'd
a)   ever want to answer that question in general and
b)   ever want to share my answer with him of all people.

I felt my throat constrict a little bit. I wondered
if I was allergic to Mark,
that way he couldn't lean socloseagainsttheprinter
on my desk and stare down expectantly
without triggering anaphylactic shock.

As I resumed typing some stupid email to some stupid travel agent about
some stupid hotel and pretended to be really contemplating the deep
and meaningful answer he wanted because
I'm just trying to get to know you better! I thought,
so let me get this straight,
my answer should be something along the lines of wildfires, or maybe
my 100% nonexistent, ambiguous life plan, or my state of early-onset
bankruptcy and quite possibly memory loss because I can't even remember
what I had for breakfast let alone why I don't know who I am
anymore or if it's only one thing
that keeps me up all night or why
I'm stuck in this office
having to answer Mark.

So let me get this straight
I said, my voice standing up on end,
You wanna know what keeps me awake?
He nodded his head slowly, condescendingly, the way
most Finance boys do, and—
Climate change.
I felt my throat constrict a little bit more.
It's sad that so many species may be extinct
by the time my kids are in their 20's.

My day was ruined and I
don't want kids I've
never
wanted kids.

Iteration (I)

In the largest quantities we share the tiniest
things—

When we kiss,
80 million microbes.

Mine

you are

Quartz so rose I can't see through
exposed veins organ
music

no churches just
Santo Spirito with all the pigeons.

Four months of voicemails
         when I couldn't, reaching you

Piazza della Signoria

I am not impatient but my hand smears
ink from pinky finger to wrist. I watch
the people, the lovers, the overweight
tourists rushing slowly with umbrellas
and fake mint gelato in waffle cones.
Sun streaks through purple-black pigeon fog.
Fake-David, complacent in mimicry,
disproves of my proximity to your
voice, which rises to me now, insistent,
like dandelions crack through the pavement
after rain. I count the crenelations.
Undici. I write faster. Forgetting,
remembering—they are the same pain. You,
the enchantment in the air of this square.

Love is exquisitely painful. I want it more than anything and I will tear open the world to get it.

—Elissa Washuta, *White Magic*

Café con Leche

5

I brush graham cracker crumbs from my firetruck shirt before playing under
the magnolia tree at the bottom of the hill. Talking to myself, still tasting milk,
I arrange stones into a fairy circle.

10

Mia takes me to the Botanical
Gardens on a Saturday in April
when my parents are too busy fighting
to see me; they offer to pay double
since she doesn't usually work on
weekends. She lives in the northeastern Bronx,
knows these fragrant winding paths like she knows
exactly how long I'll behave without
a snack. We watch the monarchs float across
azalea bush oceans, pollinate
blues, yellows, reds, pinks, purples, practice for
their migration come September. I think
of how she will leave soon, go south with the
fleetingly strong monarchs, ir a casa.

14

Padre nuestro, que estas en los cielos,
hallowed be teaching hormonal high schoolers
You're Worth Waiting For!
without offering condoms or any
useful advice. We sneak out of Spanish, stick
shiny-sloganed red stickers on boys' lockers
we think are cute, the ones we think
are worth un-waiting for.
We think very little.

20

Later
years & years
Italian dinner:

Mia   my mom   me
Me dressed
not   gay
dressed

    sweater earrings   boots
    dressed the salad
    oil   vinegar   me
    The right man is out   there
    worth waiting for. I nod.

23

Mia's husband dies. I call her.
We talk about Quito, her home; we talk of

graham crackers & milk, of the lazy iguanas
she can see from her window

stationed like stones en la plaza,
sunning themselves

into immovable.

Dirty Laundry

That bored car thing.
I stick my eyes onto one tree
until my head hurts.

Thanks to yet another holiday party
where family stand alone together and pretend to eat.

I hope inflatable Frosty pops
next time they plug in the extension cord.

Thanks to knowing getting older
is measured only by a shrinking.

Thanks to my grandfather who asks why I would give him a book
written by someone who doesn't believe in God.

Thanks to the Roman Catholic Church for leading its flock
to reject Hawking's *Brief Answers to the Big Question*s.

Thanks to *If you don't have religion
you don't have a life.*

Thanks to families who flaunt blow-up lawn decorations,
their front yards a deflated graveyard for what appears to be
piles of dirty laundry.

Christmas is almost over, thank god—
we're supposed to.

Tradycja

My mother screams somewhere
in our basement I know a mouse is dead

preoccupied with the eventual death
of my very-much-so-alive grandmother

metal springs catch my father's thumbs as they
fail to engineer an inescapable hierarchy:

flower arrangements
stainless-steel polished urns

how my grandmother argued with my mother
about lipstick

we can't resist trying to make death polished
her Polish face austerely cold

I wonder if anyone wearing black noticed
my great-grandmother wearing *coral red*

or if my great-grandfather smelled
the basement on Babci

the mouse preoccupied with
peanut-buttered traps

Zero Beach

after dusk catching ghost crabs
these glowing orbs of eight scuttling legs
using dollar store plastic nets that always broke
from my exuberance or Steve Irwin-like harmony
with the natural world

always too much sugar before a night adventure
lemon squares for me
chocolate ice cream for you
doused in mushroom clouds of bug spray
walked one   two   three   hours down the beach
flashlights making shadows rivaling moon glow
against the palm trees

until crabs left sand hole safety for hunger's sake to
navigate purling high tide hoping they didn't die
or meet a five-year-old whose favorite time of day
was night
and had eaten too much sugar
in a place where nothing ever happens unless you're
a child with a vivid imagination
retired
or a minor league baseball player

wielding a potential weapon
to a creature smaller than a cereal bowl
(though we meant no harm)

all for sand fleas or other salty bites floating
nearby depending on the ocean's generosity.

Berlin

I landed with the flu, in the wrong
town, at the wrong airport. It was more Hanover
than Berlin. I was more dead
than alive.

Holding myself up against the scratchy
carpeted seat on a bus huffing four hours
to Berlin. *Auf Nimmer!*
The Wall with its starvation, its war, its kiss

of death, on a background much the same.
Kilos of grey weigh on the air, press
Misery's shoulders as she walks
the East Gallery, the flu

in her luggage & sneakers soaked through
from rain puddles outside Berliner Dom.
I am the gold angel with her head
in her hands,

mourning wooden sarcophagi
& their pretense: adornment of the dead
over regard for the living, over
vigilance of breath above the

crypt. The austerity is severe,
it is frozen in brocade, it is
punishing—
a single whisper of the sheer

extravagance of it all & this
dynastic monolith, sham
of a tomb, would cave in again.
My spine iced-in
from the rain; I could barely move.

Ach, du. Berlin was not made for a Jew.
A gay Jew! The gay American Jew in Berlin
with the flu. You again. The ancestry
aching to be seen through the fog, the black rain.
This city won't do, not you again.

Iteration (II)

Months in churches
with you; rose music. See-through quartz

all four pigeons. When reaching Santo Spirito
I just
   exposed the tiniest things:
we couldn't kiss. Can't. So.

No voicemails.
We share organs veins

the largest quantities of mine—
80 million microbes—

you. I.

Erasure
Using two pages of unknown novel

Poor man!
    Jew

                            mischief brewing;
                be circumspect.

        strange

                        wretched, wretched
                    creature,
                one   Jew and
one   mis-
taken,
        Jew s
    are   abominably bad!

    Jew s.
        a lucky mistake;

Jew s,

        fool's

                                      my fam-

ily,
                my future resentment;

The girl becoming a woman knocks over the ketchup

& it rattles the metal outdoor table. It's a humid summer morning at their favorite breakfast place. No one looks up from steamy egg and cheese sandwiches. No one makes a sound.

I. Her Father
yells because it's the only way he knows how to
    A.   care
    B.   communicate

II. Caring
is a mix of
    A.   shame
    B.   vulnerability
    C.   what you learn from your parents
    D.   and love
    E.   or love
which all end the same

III.   No one knows anything
    A.   but they can make it seem like they know things
    B.   which is the definition of becoming an adult
        a.   Adult: an individual who has accepted they will never have anything figured out
        b.   Becoming: to simultaneously arrive as a whole & as a part

IV.   He yells at her because
    A.   he could never hurt her
        a.   Hurting: to enter the new hole in your heart with arms raised, to better reinforce its walls against caving in
            i.   You dig the hole yourself
        b.   Hurting: to cause physical harm or pain to; to injure
            i.   Done only through an action, not words
        c.   Hurting: wishing
            i.   he would leave instead
    B.   yelling is better than running away
        a.   from himself
        b.   it releases anger
            i.   venting is productive
        c.   and actions speak louder than words
    C.   he knows more than she does & wants her to listen

    a.   so she doesn't end up like him
    b.   so he doesn't have to repeat himself
    c.   so he feels like a parent
        i.   Parent: someone who teaches you that the capability to feel happiness is lost the moment you refuse to live inside your sadness
    d.   so she knows how much he loves her
        i.   enough to make her hate him

The ketchup fell over when she smacked the bottle with her hand. Her father's eyes widened as he watched her recognize herself & the girl finally understood how a

V.   Woman
    A. nobody
    B. can walk away

Wicked City

I spot a doe by blinking through my platform neighbor's
Marlboro smoke. She is oblivious, eating her greens,
doesn't chide me for staring. The air: bleach
cold.

I always sit second to last car, fourth row, left
side, aisle seat. The world tuned out besides
intermittent *This is the train to—*

She doesn't have shoes, the hunched woman
with her socks and pigeons and
her knees pulled into her chest.

Every day I walk sixteen blocks up
Madison and pass her on 58th. The Pigeon Lady,
I call her. I never even ask
her name; I never place scrunched-up singles
in the coffee tin between her sock-wrapped feet.

She is on my right. Her good eye,
the left one, stares down like a mother
at a newborn: she is completely absorbed
in how the pigeons, unafraid, let her pick them up.
They perch, hop from one hand
to the other
to the ground, flutter
back up, pecking at seeds.

This exchange seems private,
like it should not be visible
here, in the middle of exhaust and horns
blaring and people ignoring her sign
that reads Anything helps. God Bless.

My commute is two hours and forty minutes.
It begins with staring into the forest beyond
where the 7:08 pulls in at 7:12 every day. It ends
with her eye patch, with her palms
held up, the pigeons eating out of her hands,
unafraid of the unknown because
what you do know

can become just as unfamiliar.

I purposely pass by her
closely, prove I haven't let this city
callous me over.

Her palm is
a crest, a thin slice of the moon
to sustain them.
White and round and—

Grand Central. The next station is

Blue sadness is sweetness cut into strips with scissors and then into little pieces by a knife, it is the sadness of reverie and nostalgia: it may be, for example, the memory of a happiness that is now only a memory, it has receded into a niche that cannot be dusted for it is beyond your reach; distinct and dusty, blue sadness lies in your inability to dust it, it is as unreachable as the sky, it is a fact reflecting the sadness of all facts.

—Mary Ruefle, *My Private Property*

Ode to Blue

I.

She asks about my weekend: where I went, who I hung out with, what I did. Excruciatingly normal office banter. I tell her it was nice, I visited my girlfriend, and before I can get to the part about playing tennis, she cuts in. *I knew it! I could totally tell.* Eyebrows raised, I don't say anything to her. I attempt to smile with closed lips but I'm sure it appears more like a grimace, so I quickly arrange my face into a look of relief that we have an understanding between us. I don't ask her what she knew because I understand her now. I nod once; twice. *So,* I say, *what did you do this weekend?*

II.

I thought so, but I wasn't gonna say anything. I smile vaguely and chuckle for good measure. She smiles but doesn't say anything. I realize it's my turn to speak and that I don't want to. We've accidentally blocked off the aisle with our shopping carts. Unsure what sort of reaction she was expecting, I weigh the thought of complimenting her intuition, as though it is up to me to make sure this exchange continues to appear pleasant—normal, even. The wheels of my cart *screeeech* as I drag it to the left so forcefully that a tomato frees itself from a plastic bag and rolls around dully. I've been silent for too long. My old teacher reddens like the tomato that's probably bruised now. I offer, *Did my khakis give it away?*

III.

You would totally wear that jean jacket! She grins so brightly and cheerily it's off-putting. *What do you mean?* I ask my friend. *Nothing!* her voice jumps *It's just,* her voice gets even higher *it just makes sense for you!* My mind glues itself to a familiar topic I've turned over for years: how we all live with the concept of belonging and ownership. I am a certain "type" of person, just like everyone is. If something belongs to me, then suddenly this object takes on my characteristics and consequently loses its own. Similarly, ownership—where once said object has belonged to enough people (I'm still unsure who decides what number "enough" is equivalent to, and the precise value of that number) who appear to be (we have no way of knowing this, after all) that particular "type" of person (forgoing the many different subdivisions that may exist within a "type," of course), the object is now owned by that group of people. This not only erases the object's characteristics, as in belonging, but erases the group's individual preferences. Maybe the individual doesn't use that object, or even like it; maybe that object has never existed in their reality.

Then you are left with a group of people, made up of unique individuals, being told they are apparently the owners of something without it ever having belonged solely to them in the first place. My friend looks uneasy, nearly nervous, because I've neglected to take ownership of the jean jacket that she believes belongs to me. I finally say, *It made sense when I bought it—it was only $15.*

IV.

A coworker tells me how annoyed she is with her boyfriend. He won't get rid of his dog that bit the neighbor's beagle; he never takes out the garbage when she asks; he gets high every Saturday. She asks if I have a boyfriend and I tell her no—I have a girlfriend. Her eyes squint a little and she smiles. She seems satisfied about something. *Honestly, you're in a better boat anyway—girls are just, you know, it's so much easier!* She smiles even wider. *Actually,* I reply, *I think difficult people are always difficult to deal with.* She stares blankly. *Yeah…* she quickly adds *you're probably right, up to a certain extent.* I wonder where this extent lies—if it is one of many chalk lines she has drawn in the driveway of her mind to play hopscotch over, or if it is more subtle yet universally defined, like how the equator is invisible but we all accept that it's there. Probably.

V.

When my girlfriend and I started dating, I noticed my dad speaking peculiarly. *How's your friend doing?* he'd ask over dinner, feigning interest. *Who?* I'd reply, genuinely confused. *You know, your frienndddd?* and he'd draw out the word for emphasis. *She's fine,* I'd say, convinced he was just being lazy, that he didn't want to tax himself with the extra syllable—*girl*—that would have to come before the *friend* part. But it kept happening. Labor Day rolled around and he asked *Are you spending the weekend up at your friend's house?* and I said *Whose house?* and he snapped *Your friend! You mentioned she lives on a lake so are you going there or not?* Not eager to argue, I said *Yes, and I'm leaving tonight.*

VI.

Can I ask you a personal question? How long have you been a lesbian? The table is suddenly silent, and all five of my coworkers look at me. I burst out into a laugh that sounds more like a cackle and immediately everyone else laughs, too, clearly relieved that I'm okay with the question, or that I'm at least going to answer it. My face reddens and I say *Why don't we talk about this outside of work.* I feel the familiar tightness in my throat. I attempt a smile. Her smile wavers and she says *Uh, okay. I was just curious because... you know...not everyone always knows when they became one, or at least I've heard that. That people don't know for a while, I mean. So I was just wondering.* Now her face is red. I answer *Maybe we can talk about it another time.* Now no one is laughing. To avoid disaster I quickly add *Because, you know, like you said, everyone is different and I wouldn't want to speak for everyone.* But that is exactly what she thinks—that I can speak for everyone: at the table, at other tables, in other cities. Because it was implied that it was my turn to speak, to provide an answer.

VII.

Are you sure? I know it's confusing, sometimes, when you're young. She stares at me so intently through shadowy brown eyes that my hands shake. *Yes, I'm very sure. I've known for a while.* My hands need something to do so I grab a palmful of sand, let it run through my fingers onto my thigh. Blood is pumping quickly through my head, echoing in my ears, and the waves sound more distant now, like they are crashing on a shore many miles from where we are. She looks away, out at the horizon; eight miles out. I'll never forget the distance because she tells me every time I visit. *You're really sure, right?* I regret telling her at all, let alone on the beach, on a perfect day, her tone is so imploring. *Yes,* I say, louder, *it's who I am.* The breeze flows stronger and the waves seem louder, too, and my body absorbs each sensation like I am a part of this continuance, like I know what it means to remain when nothing else does, just as these waves and this breeze will break and gust long after the earth has emptied itself. Now her hands need something to do so her right reaches for the delicate gold crucifix around her neck, a piece of jewelry she never takes off, thumb and index finger rubbing like she wants to summon a genie. The tide comes in, out. In, out. In, out. Then: *Well, that might change.*

they say this woman being twisted by sleep
began to hear things
as if the sea itself leaned over her bed
she could hear they say the exact note
in which a diver twizzles like a mobile
among triangular hanged fish
and the sea wall and the weakening cliffs
as far as the hem of her clothes

        being eaten away

—Alice Oswald, *Nobody*

Conscious Blue

Breasts
Internalized homophobia
Your breasts
Drunk people glaring at us in the diner while we shared a milkshake
Same side of the booth
                                                          my hand on your thigh
The milkshake was too watery, like chocolate milk
                            is it really that hard to make a good milkshake?
Your perfectly unfurrowed eyebrows when you sleep
Skin glow in the untucked morning
You, always sleeping on your stomach
                          you aren't supposed to let infants sleep on their stomach
Kids never seem to like me
I don't want kids
                                      why would anyone want that?
The woman breastfeeding on the downtown 6

```
S     t     r        l     breasts
  y     e     i     a
    m m           c
```

                                                 hers were
                          is my left boob bigger than my right?
I'm supposed to be body positive
                                                      okay, body
Easier to hate yourself than to hate someone else
Anxiety feels like an excuse
                          There are a lot of weak people in this world
My dad sees exactly what he wants to see
                                        straight, feminine, polite
We all do
Nothing should surprise us
Focusing on colors to calm down
                                    name all the colors in the room
Anxiety is a disorder, like your brain is too messy
Are people really so afraid of owning their mistakes
                                                            white tile
                                                            blue bottle

That they convince themselves they're doing fine?
                                              white white white

Is anyone actually fine or do we just say that?
                                              white walls white tile

People are weak

                                              It just didn't work out
                                    Everything happens for a reason
We don't want to admit we weren't good enough

                                                                           I'm fine
Shame
Slut shaming

                                             even I do that sometimes
Most people do things they hate
I hate hypocrites
I'm a hypocrite

                                             everyone is in their own way
I hate poems that talk about the speaker being a poet
I hate poems that acknowledge they're a poem
Everyone thinks they're important

                                          all artists die by their own light
Crying in the Van Gogh museum
The sex worker's red dress in Amsterdam
How she threw that water bottle at British tourists for taking her photo
The arc of the liquid glowing neon red

                                  I always take showers that are too hot
Getting cat-called in Italy
It made me feel sexy

                                            I'd never tell anyone that
Easy to be a good person
Easy to be a bad person

                                                          don't dwell
There are no good or bad people, there are just people
That's bullshit

                                                                 is it?
How deep does your conscience go?
Like a little machine always running
Hums in the back of your head

                                    do good do good do good do good
How far have my legs carried me?
                                   I only liked the cat-calling that wasn't gross
Must be a big number

                                   my ass looked great when I ran track
I haven't exercised in so long
What a waste of time

                                                      On your mark...

How many miles?

                                                                   I suck at math

Thinking about math gives me anxiety

                                                                           Set...

So many things give me anxiety
I need a vacation
The beach in Puerto Rico
You're afraid to dive under waves
I love you more for your weird fears

                                      your irrational fear of seagulls

The homeless man who asked for my pineapple
I spent $18 every day for five days

                                                                        it was worth it

On a piña colada
Just because they poured it into a pineapple
White privilege
If you like piña coladas

                                                        I should get out soon

And getting caught in the   r

                              a

                 i

                       n

The smell after a rain shower

                            I should write a poem about the things
                                   I think about in the shower

Grapefruit

With all these little spots, the only fair
Comparison is the sun. Consider
Its weight, too—how it bends my wrist towards
The table, firm and cool in my palm. Gold-
Orange, the color I would've painted
My room if we hadn't always rented.
My thumb caresses its circumference;
Then, the inevitable slice through the
Equator, gentle yet insistent blade.
My neck strains to inhale the scent like it
Bows into place between your thighs. I halve
Each half, then halve each quarter, slowly sneak
My index finger above rind, under
Citrus-flesh, freeing each fragrant section.

Iteration (III)

Four churches, no voicemails:

                organ music

of 80 million microbes.

Pigeons in the largest quantities; when you are
Mine.

I couldn't share
Santo Spirito

so when we kiss—
        all the tiniest things.

Months reaching you. Quartz I just can't see through.
We, with rose-exposed veins.

Because even Titanic sunk

and that's how Fabrizio died, poor
bastard: the metallic taste of smokestack
in his lungs, *con niente,*
the scene a ball of baitfish. I imagine
being schizophrenic before Seroquel
was like the fifteenth of April, 1912.
All that noise,

then nothing.

Don't Tell Me It's Cliché

I want to retire at 55 & grow fat & spend my time
painting watercolors of mountainscapes that are actually
just hues of your breasts.

I want to grow fat & sleep late, ride
a tandem bike to Whole Foods,
beat the early-morning crowd.

I want to spend my time writing long poems
about your short temper.

You'll teach me words like *octogenarian* &
multiplicitist & things like
patience
on occasion.

You'll joke *We just went dyke riding*,
not bike riding, as I unpack boxes of
chickpea pasta, a mango ripe
& juicy enough to attract a trail of pin ants
across the kitchen counter, a fresh bundle of kale
larger than your head.

And then you'll kiss the back of my head, wrap your arms
around my waist from behind and tell me
I look good for my age, almost *too* good.

Pastoral

Some days during summer my mom and I ride our bikes down to the farm. We swoop one mile and a quarter past the empty field of weeds flattened by lounging deer, past *those redneck neighbors* with their unkempt lawn, complete with smelly chicken coop, three Pygmy goats, and abandoned pickup rusting away.

Down the steep hill—cautiously for me, recklessly for my 59-year-old mother who blurs by me, sans-helmet, yelling like she's on a rollercoaster. Past the people who tried to grow hops four years ago, tall wooden supports still upright in their yard, marking the spot where the air starts to smell of manure.

Up the tinier hill. Daffodils swaying at the crest by #24's mailbox. Wind whips our faces on the descent, nearly drowning out *Watch out, car coming!* The familiarly high-pitched whoooosh in my ears. To the right: decadently green hills, postcard-fake they're so lush, lulling up two tiers, stacked with houses.

Two red barns and a looming white silo. Quads burning now, cows rewarding us with their innocent and unaffected faces, their sandpaper tongues, their frolicking, jumpy calves all stout and square as an end table. They graze, committed proletarians, the sound like a bellows blowing into a fire. Number 46 lifts her head from the grass and walks toward me.

She has your eyes, I think to myself. Then I think this is an absurd thing to think, but she does; 46 looks at me intently yet gently, saunters by, decides to eat in the far-right corner of the field. I want to keep this a secret between the three of us—you, me, and 46, because I figure anyone else would probably laugh. But I'm no good at secrets, at least not my own.

I tell my mom 46 has your eyes. She smiles. *I don't know why,* I say. *Well, I like 27. She looks fat and happy,* she replies. We get back on our bikes, the black Schwinn she gave my dad in '92 as a birthday gift and the purple one she bought for herself the next day, realizing my dad would never bike alone.

Self-Portrait

The kobudai came back in winter. She
Survives her own blue death swimming through my
Yard, her forehead leaving miniscule drifts
In the snow. She looks at me, looks cold and
Bruised as the week-old apple in my fridge,
Looks astounded to find me sunken here,
So far from the sea. It occurs to me
To pour two cups of tea—one with honey,
One without. The window fogs up. I write
Who are you? in the condensation. Hours
Or a minute pass. The glass clear, I see
She's carefully carved one word in the snow:
L o o k. I see him now; high cheekbones, thin lips.
Hazel eyes. I feel his scaly skin: mine.

You've Reached the Dykes II

We live in a home where it is quiet, other than the wind and the sea. Seashells make up the driveway and there is an aloe vera plant on the windowsill behind our kitchen sink. When it rains a tiny hole in the ceiling of our bathroom drips, forming a yellow ring around the drain of the tub as the water pools. I am always the one who scrubs it away and I let you know this. You let me know that I shouldn't say "always" unless it comes before the words "love you" and after "I will." If we argue sometimes, we hardly notice. If we make love all the time, it is never enough. Sometimes I walk around barefoot in my underwear to turn you on. I make Italian food a lot and you let me know this, because it is a good thing. This is a good thing to know because I thought you were trying not to eat bread. Trying and failing, you say. I laugh. Our home is full of laughter. Laughing is what makes a house a home; a house has silent things in it and silent people who hang around like the ugly paintings on its walls. We have paintings but they were painted by us in the class we take together every other weekend. Mine are the ugliest, except for the painting of a crimson sunset. Yours are beautifully sad like the look you get sometimes when you are somewhere else and also in front of me.

Veronica Schorr received the 2018-2019 Collins Literary Prize in Poetry. Her poems and nonfiction have appeared in *Long River Review* and *Chronogram*. Schorr is Assistant Poetry Editor at *EcoTheo Review*, a reviewer for New York Journal of Books, and a writer for Witness Change. She currently lives in Connecticut. *Conscious Blue* is her debut chapbook.

www.ingramcontent.com/pod-product-compliance
Lightning Source LLC
LaVergne TN
LVHW041552070426
835507LV00011B/1060